Steven
Spielberg

Other titles in the Inventors and Creators series include:

Steven
Spielberg

Adam Woog

**KIDHAVEN
PRESS**™

San Diego • Detroit • New York • San Francisco • Cleveland
New Haven, Conn. • Waterville, Maine • London • Munich

To Nahnie Freemanson and her 2001–2002 students in Room 202 at Olympic View Elementary School in Seattle, Washington. Thanks for the help!

On the cover: Director Steven Spielberg works with his crew on the set of the film *Saving Private Ryan*.

Picture Credits

Cover Photo: © AFP/CORBIS
© AFP/CORBIS, 40
© Associated Press, AP, 15
© Associated Press/Fashion Wire Daily, 28
© W. Cody/CORBIS, 10
© CORBIS, 12
© Hulton/Archive by Getty Images, 7, 13, 21, 22, 29
© The Kobal Collection, 11, 18, 20, 24, 36
© Robert Landau/CORBIS, 17
© Photo B.D.V./CORBIS, 26
© Reuters NewMedia Inc./CORBIS, 31, 34, 37, 39
© Peter Turnley/CORBIS, 30

For more information, contact
KidHaven Press
27500 Drake Rd.
Farmington Hills, MI 48331-3535
Or you can visit our Internet site at http://www.gale.com

LIBRARY OF CONGRESS CATALOGING-IN-PUBLICATION DATA

Woog, Adam, 1953-
  Steven Spielberg / by Adam Woog.
     p. cm. — (Inventors and creators series)
Includes bibliographical references and index.
  Summary: Discusses the life and work of Steven Spielberg, to include childhood; directing and producing; movies; family; and achievements.
     ISBN 0-7377-1418-2 (hard : alk. paper)
  1. Spielberg, Steven, 1947—-Juvenile literature. 2. Motion picture producers and directors—United States—Biography—Juvenile literature. I. Title. II. Series.
PN1998.3.S65 W66 2003
791.43'0233'092—dc21

                                                                    2002007608

Printed in China

Contents

Hollywood Legend

Steven Spielberg is the most successful film **director** in the world. His movies are wildly popular. More people have seen and enjoyed Spielberg movies than those of any other director in history. As a result, many of his films are among the movie world's top moneymakers.

Spielberg's movies are not just popular moneymakers, however. They are also wonderfully creative.

The list of Spielberg's movies is very long. Three of his most famous are *Raiders of the Lost Ark*, *E.T. the Extra-Terrestrial*, and *Jurassic Park*. Each stands out because it is highly imaginative, tells an exciting story, and uses thrilling images.

The Secret of His Success

One reason for Spielberg's success is his gift for making dazzling images. This is possible partly because he understands every aspect of making a movie, from costumes to camera work and editing.

Even more important is his ability to connect with audiences. He imagines that he is the audience, and makes

Director Steven Spielberg creates films that the audience can relate to and easily understand.

movies that he wants to see himself. Spielberg comments, "I've made movies that are bigger than life and movies that haven't happened to me, but stories that I wish would happen to me and characters I wish I could be more like."[1]

Spielberg's films are successful also because they have simple messages that almost anyone can understand. The characters in them are usually ordinary people in extraordinary situations. Audiences find it easy to relate to such everyday heroes.

Spielberg's Top $ Makers

Year	Film	Money Made
1982	E.T. the Extra-Terrestrial	$426,971,134
1993	Jurassic Park	$357,067,947
1975	Jaws	$261,225,440
1981	Raiders of the Lost Ark	$242,374,454
1997	The Lost World: Jurassic Park	$229,086,679
1998	Saving Private Ryan	$216,335,085
1989	Indiana Jones and the Last Crusade	$197,171,806
1984	Indiana Jones and the Temple of Doom	$179,870,271
1977	Close Encounters of the Third Kind	$166,000,000
1991	Hook	$119,654,824

The director also has a gift for turning events from his personal life, such as childhood joys and fears, into exciting or emotional scenes. Indiana Jones's fear of snakes is one example. As a child, Spielberg really was afraid of snakes.

Spielberg often uses events from his own family life in his movies. The director's mother, Leah Spielberg, remarks, "You are viewing our family at the dinner table when you see *E.T.*"[2]

Spielberg has a special gift for connecting with children. Kids are usually a big part of his audience. Adults also enjoy Spielberg's movies. They enjoy both the grown-up and kid parts. Writer Martin Amis notes, "By now a billion Earthlings have seen his films. They have only one thing in common. They have all, at some stage, been children."[3]

Spielberg has always been interested in telling exciting stories. His love affair with the movies began early in life.

Chapter One

Growing Up

Steven Allan Spielberg was born on December 18, 1946, in Cincinnati, Ohio. He was the first child of Arnold and Leah Spielberg.

Arnold and Leah had very different interests and personalities. Arnold Spielberg was a serious and often cold man. He was an engineer in the brand-new field of computer technology. Leah Spielberg had a good sense of humor and a creative, artistic side. She liked lively conversation and was a talented piano player.

Steven shares parts of his personality with both parents. From his father, he picked up an interest in science. From his mother, he inherited a creative side.

The director also has his mother's ability to get along with people. On a movie set, he is usually friendly and even-tempered with everyone. As a private person, he is known to be shy, kind, and considerate.

Steven was a bright and curious child. His family joked that his first word was "why?" However, he was an average student and mostly got Cs in school. Arnold nagged his son to study harder, but Leah was more tolerant.

Cincinnati, Ohio is Steven Spielberg's birthplace.

Always Moving

The Spielbergs were part of a close-knit family that included Steven's grandparents on both sides. Soon after Steven's birth, however, Arnold changed jobs and the family left this warm environment for New Jersey.

The Spielbergs moved again several times after that. Steven was shy, and each time had trouble making new friends. Leaving familiar places behind is a frequent theme in his movies. Spielberg recalls, "Just as I'd become accustomed to a school and a teacher and a best friend, the FOR SALE sign would dig into the front lawn."[4]

When Steven was ten, the family moved to Scottsdale, Arizona. Arizona was very different from what Steven was used to. It was hot and dry. There were strange new sights, such as pick-up trucks and men with cowboy hats. Also, the Arizona desert scared Steven. It was full of strange creatures, like lizards, and equally strange plants, like cactuses.

Arnold Spielberg liked the desert, however, and often took his family on camping trips. On one occasion, Arnold woke his son at night and drove into the desert to watch a dramatic meteor shower.

This was an important moment for Steven. His father explained the event in scientific terms, but Steven also saw it as beautiful and mysterious. He later used his memory of the event to create a famous movie moment: the episode in *Close Encounters of the Third Kind* when people gather at night to watch UFOs.

Early Entertainment

Steven saw his first movie when he was six. It was *The Greatest Show on Earth*, a circus spectacular. He loved it. After that, Steven was eager to see all the movies he could, and rarely missed the Saturday kids' matinee at the local theater.

People gather to watch UFOs in a scene from Spielberg's film *Close Encounters of the Third Kind.*

Steven loved other kinds of entertainment as well. He was crazy about comic books, for instance—especially Superman, Batman, and Donald Duck.

However, television was the biggest part of Steven's early entertainment. TV was just becoming a part of American life in the early 1950s. Steven was in the first generation to have TV as part of everyday life.

All television thrilled him. He loved westerns, situation comedies, police shows, and Disney specials. His father limited the amount of time he could spend watching TV, but Steven figured out a way to watch more.

Arnold used to put a hair over the controls of the TV. If the hair was moved, he would know his son was watching when it was forbidden. However, Steven would memorize the position of the hair, watch secretly, then replace it exactly.

Steven also made his own entertainment. He especially liked to frighten his three younger sisters with spooky sto-

A boy reads a Superman comic book just as Spielberg did when he was a child.

Director Steven Spielberg works on the set of *E.T. the Extra-Terrestrial* in 1982.

ries and weird games. Once, after the Spielberg kids had seen a movie about a Martian who kept a human head in a fishbowl, he terrified his sisters by locking them in a closet with a fishbowl. Spielberg says that such tricks reflected his own fears of monsters and other things.

Home Movies

The first Spielberg films were very simple. They were home movies that Steven shot with his family's twenty-dollar, **eight-millimeter** camera. At first he simply recorded family outings, like camping trips. Soon, however, Steven was creating his own stories on film, starring family and friends.

He liked to make westerns, comedies, mysteries, and war movies. Steven began spending most of his allowance money and spare time on making movies. His hobby quickly became an obsession.

Steven was especially good at creating special effects. He discovered that flour, kicked up by an actor, could fake a bomb explosion. Once, in the kitchen, Steven blew up a pressure cooker full of cherries while making pretend blood and gore. His mother said that she was still finding bits of the mess for years afterward.

In high school, Steven made *Escape to Nowhere*, a forty-minute, silent World War II adventure. It won first place in a statewide contest. The prizes included a good camera and a library of books about film. To go with these treasures, Steven's father bought him a new projector and sound system.

Another Move and a Broken Home

Steven's first full-length film, made in 1964, was a science fiction story, *Firelight*. It was about a UFO expert tracking an alien. The alien kidnaps a girl, played by Steven's sister Nancy.

Steven rented a local movie theater for the showing. The show sold out, thanks to the family and friends of his crew and cast. He made a small profit beyond the six hundred dollars *Firelight* had cost him.

That year the Spielbergs moved yet again. This time it was to Saratoga, near San Jose, California. Steven finished high school there.

This was not a happy time for Steven. Athletes and surfers dominated the social life at Saratoga High. They tormented Steven because he was an outsider. They made fun of his awkward appearance, his interest in movies, and his Jewish religion. Spielberg recalls of those years, "I was the weird, skinny kid with the acne. I was a wimp."[5]

Worse, there was tension in the Spielberg home. Leah and Arnold were unhappy together. Around the time

Steven Spielberg accepts a Lifetime Achievement award in 2002. Spielberg's poor high school grades ultimately did not hinder his success.

Steven graduated, they separated. They divorced the next year. The breakup deeply saddened Steven.

Steven graduated from high school with a C average. His grades were not good enough to get into a university with a film department. Instead, in 1967 he started college in Long Beach, California. He chose that school because it was close to Hollywood. Having the famous movie capital nearby, he thought, would help him learn everything he needed to know about the movies.

Chapter Two

The Moviemaker

In college, Spielberg often ignored his classes. Instead, he spent his days watching movies in the theaters and his nights watching television. One summer, he got a job at Universal Studios. He avidly watched the professionals making TV shows and movies.

Spielberg also worked at odd jobs, such as cafeteria work, to make money for his own movies. He constantly bugged movie studio executives to look at his work. And finally he got lucky. One of his short films impressed Sidney Sheinberg, Universal Television's vice president for production.

Sheinberg saw Spielberg's talent. He also liked how hard Spielberg worked, and how much he already knew about movies. In 1968, Sheinberg offered Steven a job directing TV programs. Spielberg immediately dropped out of college to take the job.

He was not a success at first. He had many ambitious ideas, and he spent a lot of time making every scene perfect. Crews working under Spielberg sometimes made fun of this. They also teased him because of his youth.

However, with each assignment his confidence grew. Also, his talent was obvious. In time, his crews were more respectful.

The First Features

The first major film that Spielberg wrote and directed was a made-for-TV movie, *Duel*. In it, the driver of a monstrous truck terrorizes a traveling salesman.

The movie was first shown in 1971. The public, the critics, and members of the entertainment industry liked its energy and its scary story. After it was broadcast, Spielberg received many offers to direct movies.

He chose an idea he was already working on. *The Sugarland Express* was based on a real event. It was about a convict who escaped from jail and led police on a cross-country chase. It was not a huge success, however. Critics liked it, but audiences did not. They were not sure if it was comedy or drama.

In order to be close to Hollywood, Spielberg got a summer job working at Universal Studios.

Jaws

While making *Sugarland*, Spielberg read a novel about a killer shark on a rampage. It scared him, and he knew it would make a terrifying (and exciting) movie.

The making of that movie, called *Jaws*, had many problems. For example, it was difficult to film scenes on

A photo depicts the huge and scary shark's teeth from a scene in the film *Jaws*.

open water. Sometimes, only a few seconds of film could be shot in an entire day.

Each day of production cost thousands of dollars for Universal, which was backing *Jaws*. The studio was unhappy and nearly closed the movie down.

Spielberg was worried and depressed by the time *Jaws* was finished. He knew that his career was over if it failed. No one would ever hire him again.

But *Jaws* was an instant hit. The intense story terrified and delighted millions. Within two months of its release in 1975, it set a new **box office** (ticket sales) record. It became the most successful film in history up to that point. It also made international stars out of Spielberg and its unknown lead actor, Richard Dreyfuss.

A Star

Previously an unknown, Spielberg could suddenly do no wrong. After *Jaws*, nearly every movie he made from the mid-1970s to the mid-1980s was a smash hit. They were all **blockbusters**—big, splashy adventure movies he called "popcorn movies."

Spielberg's blockbusters each told an exciting story. Also, each used lots of special effects. This was not always good, some critics said. They complained that Spielberg used so many special effects that he lost sight of simple storytelling about human characters.

His most successful movie, creatively and financially, was a good balance of special effects and an excellent human story. *E.T. the Extra-Terrestrial* began as an idea very close to Spielberg's own heart.

E.T. and actor Henry Thomas share a tender moment in Spielberg's 1982 blockbuster, *E.T. the Extra-Terrestrial.*

In the early 1980s, Spielberg was making the first Indiana Jones movie in North Africa. He was lonely being so far away from friends and family. He comforted himself the same way he had in his childhood: He invented an imaginary friend. In this case, it was a warm-hearted alien.

Calling Home

With the help of a screenwriter, Melissa Mathison, Spielberg turned his idea into a movie script. In their version, the alien was a botanist stranded on Earth. His human friend was a boy who came from a broken home. The boy was a lot like Spielberg himself.

The tender relationship between these two was the heart of *E.T.* Spielberg called it "a love story, the love between a ten-year-old boy and a nine-hundred-year-old alien."[6]

When the movie was released in 1982, audiences and critics responded powerfully to its simple, clear message—

a message of love, peace, and hope mixed with sadness. It quickly became the biggest box office hit in history.

E.T.'s message earned Spielberg several important honors. He was invited to screen the film for the president of the United States and for the queen of England. Also, officials at the United Nations gave the director a special peace medal.

E.T. was, in many ways, typical of the movies Spielberg made during this period. It mixed elements of science with magic and wonder. Its story was a thrilling adventure, and it stressed the importance of friendship, love, and family.

The Blockbuster Era

Not all of Spielberg's movies from this period were successful. For example, his comedy *1941* was a major flop. It was based on a true event: the reactions of panic-stricken

Steven Spielberg points to something in the distance as he directs actor Henry Thomas in a scene from *E.T.*

Actor Harrison Ford became famous for his role as the adventurous and death-defying hero Indiana Jones.

Californians in the early days of World War II. Critics and audiences felt uncomfortable with a comedy based on such a serious subject.

This was an exception, however. Usually, Spielberg made hit after hit. He became known as Hollywood's wonder child—a young genius who could do no wrong.

In less than a decade, from *Jaws* in 1975 to *Indiana Jones and the Temple of Doom* in 1984, Spielberg had gone from Hollywood nobody to Hollywood king. He changed the course of moviemaking, by helping to create the age of the blockbuster. After Spielberg's run of hits, many directors tried to make similar, flashy movies.

Spielberg could easily have continued making big "popcorn movies," but he did not want to. He did not give them up, but he also wanted to start making more thoughtful, serious films.

Chapter Three

The Storyteller Matures

Spielberg's next movie, a version of Alice Walker's prize-winning novel *The Color Purple*, reflected this change in his feelings. It was completely unlike the spectaculars that had made the director famous.

The Color Purple, released in 1985, is a serious story. Its main character is Celie, a poor black woman in rural Georgia early in the twentieth century. The novel deals with intense subjects such as abuse, prejudice, and racial identity.

Spielberg was moved by the book's message. As a teenager he had felt like an outsider, and he had experienced discrimination because he was Jewish.

Still, many people wondered if Spielberg could do a good job. After all, he was a white, Jewish male who was known for making adventure movies.

Even Spielberg was not sure. One day, he was talking to Quincy Jones, one of the movie's **producers**. When Spielberg expressed his doubts, Jones reassured him: "You didn't have to come from Mars to do *E.T.*, did you?"[7]

A Balance

In spite of the doubts, Spielberg made a moving and entertaining picture. Much of *The Color Purple*'s success came from its powerful performances. These included two unknown actors making their first film appearances: Oprah Winfrey and Whoopi Goldberg.

During the next period of his career, Spielberg balanced small films with big ones. Not all were huge successes. However, each showed that he was maturing as a filmmaker. All of them had themes that were important to him. Among these were family ties, survival in difficult conditions, and the pain of growing up.

Steven Spielberg directs actress Whoopi Goldberg in *The Color Purple.*

At the same time that his moviemaking matured, Spielberg's private life matured. The director had often described himself as an overgrown kid. He had always been too obsessed with moviemaking to have a serious relationship. Now, however, he started settling into the adult responsibilities of being a husband and father.

Private Life

Actress Amy Irving was Spielberg's first serious girlfriend. They had met while he was working on *Close Encounters*.

It was always a troubled romance. In part this was because Amy felt stifled. She worried that other people in Hollywood thought of her only as Steven's girlfriend, rather than an actress recognized for her own talents.

Despite their troubles, the couple married in 1985 and had a son, Max. Spielberg tried hard to be a family man. Though he still worked long hours, he cut down somewhat on his nonstop work schedule. Meanwhile, his wife was trying to maintain her own career.

The pressures of merging their busy schedules finally became too great. After three and a half years, Amy and Steven announced their divorce.

Spielberg was brokenhearted. He had always wanted a stable family, and he hated the idea of repeating his parents' divorce. He has remarked that the two most difficult events in his life were their breakup and his own.

Another Marriage

Soon, however, the director had a new romance. She was Kate Capshaw, who had played Willie in *Indiana Jones*

Amy Irving and Steven Spielberg hold their son Max in a photograph taken shortly before the couple divorced.

and the Temple of Doom. After a long period of courtship, she and Spielberg were married in 1991.

She and Steven were both interested in having a large family. Each already had one child from a first marriage: Max from Steven's and Jessica from Kate's. Kate adopted another child, Theo, before their marriage. They now have four more—Sasha, Sawyer, Destry, and Mikaela—for a total of seven.

Perhaps because of this newfound stability, Spielberg's next projects were two of his best. They represented his twin desires: to make both entertaining blockbusters and serious, thought-provoking dramas.

Jurassic Park

First came the blockbuster. *Jurassic Park* posed a fascinating question: What if scientists could create living dinosaurs from ancient DNA?

Once again, Spielberg used a fast-paced story to explore some serious topics. Among these were father figures, children in danger, and the ways in which technology can both help and hurt humankind.

Given the subject matter and Spielberg's reputation, it was no surprise that the movie was a smash hit when it opened in 1993. Within four months, Spielberg broke his own box office record. Up until then, the champion had been *E.T.*

Spielberg's other film from 1993 was a serious drama. *Schindler's List* was based on a true story about Oskar Schindler, a non-Jewish businessman who secretly rescued Jews from concentration camps during World War II. These Jews were about to be killed as part of the **Holocaust**, the massacre of millions by German Nazis.

Spielberg and his wife Kate Capshaw pose in New York in 2002. They were married in 1991 after a long courtship.

Adolf Hitler salutes his troops. Spielberg made the movie *Schindler's List* to help his children understand Hitler's murder of millions during the Holocaust.

Schindler's List

For years, Spielberg had thought about making a Holocaust movie. For a long time, however, the idea had been too painful. Several members of his family had been killed during the war.

What changed his mind was starting a family of his own. He says he wanted his children to understand their ancestors. "I got interested for the sake of my children, [for] when they got old enough to ask me questions like,

Steven Spielberg and wife Kate Capshaw walk through the Auschwitz concentration camp in Poland in 1994.

'Dad, where did you come from? Where did Grandma come from?'"[8]

The making of *Schindler's List* was a difficult experience for Spielberg. He had never been very religious. While making the movie, however, he began to change. He was flooded with powerful emotions.

Shooting the film in Poland was especially draining. Spielberg says he cried every day and felt frightened all the time. He remembered stories from his childhood about family and friends who had been lost during the war.

Fortunately, the director had strong support. His family stayed with him, and his parents and rabbi visited. Sometimes he phoned his friend Robin Williams in California. Williams would spend half an hour or more cheering up his faraway friend with comedy skits.

A Triumph

Because of its serious topic, no one expected *Schindler's List* to be popular. Spielberg did not even expect it to

In an appearance before Congress, Steven Spielberg passionately testifies about hate crimes.

make a profit. It had simply been a statement he needed to make.

To everyone's surprise, the movie was an enormous hit. Millions of people were moved by its message. It renewed public awareness around the world about the Holocaust.

Furthermore, *Schindler's List* finally got Spielberg formal recognition from his Hollywood colleagues. Although he was one of Hollywood's most popular and successful artists, his movies had never won a major Academy Award (that is, for best director or picture). Some observers felt he had been unfairly snubbed by the film industry.

Now, however, he finally was given this honor. *Schindler's List* swept the 1993 Oscars. It won in seven categories, including Best Director and Best Picture. Spielberg was thrilled to receive these awards.

He was exhausted, however, after making *Schindler's List* and *Jurassic Park* back-to-back. He decided to take time off. He did not begin any full-time movie projects for three years.

Chapter Four

Balancing Work and Family

The biggest project Spielberg worked on during his time off was the creation of a new company, DreamWorks SKG. It was a major studio for film, TV, and music production. To form it, Spielberg joined with two other entertainment giants: Jeffrey Katzenberg, who was once chairman of Walt Disney Studios, and David Geffen, a music producer. (The initials "SKG" stand for their last names.)

But Spielberg did not work too hard during this "retirement." Mostly, he spent time with his family.

Even though he had long been the world's most successful and popular film director, earlier in his life Steven had sometimes experienced feelings of loneliness and insecurity. His marriage to Kate has apparently changed that. By all accounts it is happy and stable.

Friends and associates agree that the marriage has made Spielberg more secure, calm, and balanced. A longtime colleague, Kathleen Kennedy, says, "He has a personal confidence now and isn't trying to prove anything to himself anymore."[9]

Steven Spielberg poses with actress Rosie Perez and his Dreamworks business partner Jeffrey Katzenberg.

During his time off, he especially wanted to enjoy watching his children as they grew up. He recalls that this was more or less a full-time job: "I was Mr. Carpool. We had breakfast and dinner together every day. It's full-time work, because every one of our kids is a leader. Seven leaders, no followers."[10]

Connecting with His Parents

In addition to spending time with his wife and children, Spielberg worked hard to create close relationships with his mother and father. Steven has always remained close to his mother, so keeping that connection was not difficult.

It was harder for Spielberg to rebuild a relationship with his father, however. Arnold and Steven Spielberg had grown apart during the tense period following the elder Spielberg's divorce.

Furthermore, Arnold had been very angry when Steven dropped out of college. He had not been able to accept Steven's chosen career path. During all of the years of Steven's success as a director, the two had remained far apart. They rarely saw or spoke with each other.

However, during his "retirement," Spielberg realized that to be a good father he needed to spend time with his own father. He reached out to Arnold Spielberg, and the two were able to connect again.

They connected so well, in fact, that Spielberg served as his father's best man when Arnold remarried. Spielberg comments about their new closeness, "It was like coming home again, making up for lost time—and we have a lot of lost time between us. Now we're so close, it's fantastic."[11]

Back to the Movies

Spielberg returned to directing with *The Lost World: Jurassic Park*. The movie was both familiar and new. It was familiar because it was a huge blockbuster.

It was new because, with the exception of the Indiana Jones films, Spielberg had never directed a sequel. (Someone else directed the sequel of *Jaws*.)

More recently, Spielberg's movies have reflected his widely varied interests. He has directed historical dramas, war movies, and science fiction and crime stories.

After taking three years off to spend time with his family, Spielberg returned to direct the 1997 blockbuster *The Lost World: Jurassic Park* (a scene from the movie, pictured).

All of them, in their own ways, explore the themes and ideas that have long fascinated the director. Among these are childhood, family, personal freedom, and what happens to people when they lose any of these.

Honors and Wealth

Spielberg has received many honors from professional organizations and governments. One of the highest of these honors was a National Humanities Medal awarded by President Bill Clinton. The director was also given a

President Bill Clinton and First Lady Hillary Clinton present Steven Spielberg with a National Humanities Medal.

knighthood from England's Queen Elizabeth. (He is not called "Sir," however, because he is not a British citizen.)

Spielberg has been a wealthy man for many years. He continues to be one of the richest people in the entertainment industry. His personal fortune is estimated at about $1 billion.

Spielberg has invested some of his profits in his production company, Amblin. He also owns several homes, including ones in Los Angeles and New York.

However, the director has also given a considerable amount of his money to worthy causes. Ever since *Jaws* made his first fortune, Spielberg has donated money to causes that he thinks are important.

For instance, he has given large sums to such organizations as Harvard University, for research into life on other planets. He has also contributed to the D-Day Memorial Foundation, the Democratic Party, and the Starbright Foundation, which helps seriously ill children. (He is also the cochairman, with General Norman Schwartzkopf, of the Starbright Foundation.)

Spielberg has one very special focus for his donations to worthy causes. He has concentrated most of his giving on Jewish causes. All of his millions of dollars in profits from *Schindler's List*, for instance, have gone to Jewish organizations and efforts. These include the Holocaust Museum in Washington, D.C., and the restoration of Anne Frank's house in Amsterdam.

Being a Kid and an Adult

Spielberg has often said that he never really grew up. He claims that he is just an overgrown kid. For instance, he is still as enthusiastic about cartoons or games as when he was very young. He says, "I'm the guy who tries to keep the kids downstairs when my wife is trying to get them to bed."[12]

Even though he is middle-aged now, he still has many characteristics left over from his childhood. For

Steven Spielberg and stepdaughter Jessica Capshaw stand for the National Anthem before a Lakers basketball game.

Steven Spielberg has received many awards for his touching and creative films.

example, he has been a lifelong nail-biter. He avoids elevators and airplanes when possible, and he sucks on a finger when thinking.

In many ways the director seems to have grown into maturity. He has a close-knit family and an outstanding body of work. He has become wealthy, and is giving away much of his money to causes he believes in. In many ways, he has certainly grown up.

Even as he has reached middle age, Spielberg has kept his boyish enthusiasm for life. This sense of wonder and excitement is the basic message of almost all his movies.

His personal life, in many ways, reflects this same basic message. The message delivers a positive, optimistic, hopeful vision of life. Millions of Spielberg fans hope that he can keep delivering this message for a long time to come.

Notes

Introduction: Hollywood Legend

1. Quoted in Roger Ebert and Gene Siskel, *The Future of the Movies*. Kansas City: Andrews & McMeel, 1991, p. 39.
2. Quoted in Donald R. Mott and Cheryl McAllister Saunders, *Steven Spielberg*. Boston: Twayne, 1986, p. 12.
3. Martin Amis, *The Moronic Inferno and Other Visits to America*. New York: Viking Penguin, 1987, p. 147.

Chapter One: Growing Up

4. Quoted in Joseph McBride, *Steven Spielberg: A Biography*. New York: Simon & Schuster, 1997, p. 47.
5. Quoted in Amis, *The Moronic Inferno*, p. 148.

Chapter Two: The Moviemaker

6. Quoted in Amis, *The Moronic Inferno*, p. 152.

Chapter Three: The Storyteller Matures

7. Quoted in Philip M. Taylor, *Steven Spielberg: The Man, His Movies and Their Meaning*. New York: Continuum, 1994, p. 113.
8. Quoted in Julie Salamon, "The Long Voyage Home," *Harper's Bazaar*, February 1994, n.p.

Chapter Four: Balancing Work and Family

9. Quoted in David Ansen, "Spielberg's Obsession," *Newsweek*, December 20, 1993, p. 112.

10. Quoted in Richard Corliss and Jeffrey Ressner, "Peter Pan Grows Up: But Can He Still Fly?" *Time*, May 19, 1997, p. 74.

11. Quoted in Corliss and Ressner, "Peter Pan Grows Up: But Can He Still Fly?," p. 74.

12. Quoted in Frank Sanello, *Spielberg: The Man, The Movies, The Mythology*. Dallas: Taylor, 1996, p. 197.

Glossary

blockbuster: A large-scale movie spectacular, often using lots of special effects.

box office: The term used to describe the ticket sales of a movie, as in "good box office."

director: The person who is responsible for the artistic direction of a movie, such as creating special effects or telling actors what to do.

eight-millimeter: A relatively simple and inexpensive form of "home" or personal movie film, popular before the widespread use of video.

Holocaust: The massacre of millions of Jews by Germany during World War II.

producer: The person who is the general supervisor of a film, overseeing such matters as budgets, casting, and locations.

For Further Exploration

Tom Collins, *Steven Spielberg: Creator of E.T.* Minneapolis: Dillon Press, 1983. A very basic book. Lists Spielberg's birth year incorrectly as 1947.

Thomas Conklin, *Meet Steven Spielberg*. New York: Random House, 1994. A brief paperback biography.

Jody Duncan, *The Making of The Lost World: Jurassic Park*. New York: Ballantine Books, 1997. A heavily illustrated peek behind the scenes of one of Spielberg's most popular movies. Written for adults, but children will like the graphics.

Elizabeth Ferber, *Steven Spielberg*. Philadelphia: Chelsea House, 1997. A well-written look at Spielberg's life and career up to *Schindler's List*.

Jim Hargrove, *Steven Spielberg: Amazing Filmmaker.* Chicago: Childrens Press, 1988. A good introduction for young adults.

Virginia Meachum, *Steven Spielberg: Hollywood Filmmaker.* Springfield, NJ: Enslow, 1996. This well-written introduction has a good filmography.

Tom Powers, *Steven Spielberg: Master Storyteller*. Minneapolis: Lerner Publications, 1997. This book about Spielberg's life has some useful documentation in its footnotes.

Susan Goldman Rubin, *Steven Spielberg: Crazy for Movies*. New York: Harry N. Abrams, 2001. A well-illustrated book.

William Schoell, *Magic Man: The Life and Films of Steven Spielberg*. Greensboro, NC: Tudor, 1998. A good short biography.

Index